The Future of Learning: Artificial Intelligence in K12 Education

AI in K-12 Education

Adam Smith

Published by A. Smith Media, 2023.

THE FUTURE OF LEARNING: ARTIFICIAL INTELLIGENCE IN K12 EDUCATION

First edition. May 30, 2023.

ISBN: 979-8223243458

Written by Adam Smith.

Also by Adam Smith

AI in K-12 Education
Intelligent Machines in the Classroom: Unlocking the Potential of AI in K12 Education
The Future of Learning: Artificial Intelligence in K12 Education
Towards an AI-Infused Revolution in K12 Education
Unleashing AI in the Classroom: Strategies for Implementing Intelligent Technologies in K-12 Education
Unleashing the Potential of Artificial Intelligence in K-12 Education: Reimagining How Learning Happens

Breaking Down Bad Habits
Breaking Down Bad Habits: How to Overcome Self-Defeating Behaviors and Achieve Success

Standalone
Brain Dead: When It Comes To Improving Mental Health, What The Hell Are We Waiting For?
40 Things Intelligent People Do Daily
The Beginner's Guide to Quantum Computing & Mechanics
Open Source AI

Watch for more at https://books2read.com/adamsmith.

Table of Contents

Chapter 1: "Leveraging AI for Enhancing the Personalized Learning Experience in the Classroom"

The idea of leveraging artificial intelligence (AI) to enhance the personalized learning experience in the classroom is an exciting prospect for many educators, as it provides the opportunity to tailor educational materials to the specific needs and capabilities of each individual student. AI can be used to track student progress, identify areas for improvement, provide personalized coaching and advice, and create a more collaborative learning environment.

Personalized learning has been shown to be more effective than traditional classroom settings, since students are able to focus on topics that they are most interested in and have the best chance of mastering. However, achieving this goal can be difficult, as teachers often have to manually track and assess student progress and provide personalized assistance.

In order to address this issue, AI technology can be leveraged for several distinct tasks. First, AI can be used to measure student progress. AI algorithms can track how well a student is understanding the material, the amount of time spent on the task, and any areas where the student is struggling or doing well. This data can then be used to provide personalized guidance to the student, helping to ensure their comprehension of the material.

AI can also provide personalized feedback and advice to students, helping them to understand their strengths and weaknesses and take steps to address any shortcomings. For example, AI could suggest focus areas for improvement, or even provide tailored practice problems for each student to practice and hone their skills in a particular area.

AI can also be leveraged to create a more collaborative learning environment. AI can be used to identify potential teammates for group projects, fostering collaboration and enhancing the on the whole learning experience. Additionally, AI can also be used to facilitate online learning, providing students with personal tutoring or even creating custom learning paths based on data collected from the students' progress.

AI can also be used to customize the classroom experience itself. AI can be used to adjust the lighting, noise levels, and classroom temperature to better suit the needs of the students, helping to ensure they are comfortable and able to focus on their learning.

Leveraging AI for enhancing the personalized learning experience in the classroom can prove to be an invaluable asset. AI can provide tailored coaching and advice, measure student progress, and create a more collaborative learning environment. Moreover, AI can also be used to customize the classroom itself. For educators looking to create a personalized learning experience for their students, the advantages that AI can bring are undeniable.

Chapter 2: "Maximizing Learning Outcomes with AI: Strategies for Personalized Instruction in the Classroom"

Artificial Intelligence (AI) has become an increasingly important tool in the modern education system. AI can be leveraged to offer personalized instruction in the classroom, allowing teachers to better monitor student progress and maximize learning outcomes. By leveraging data to understand a student's strengths and weaknesses, AI can help teachers to better prepare lesson plans to provide a personalized learning experience.

To maximize learning outcomes and apply AI in the classroom, it is important for teachers to have an understanding of what AI is and the capabilities it can offer. AI consists of various technologies and algorithms which can be used to recognize, analyze, and process data to form insights that enable better decision-making. When applied to classroom instruction, AI can be used to enhance student understanding and engagement by tailoring an individual's learning experience.

An effective way to use AI to personalize instruction is by incorporating adaptive learning into the classroom. Adaptive learning is an AI-driven approach that monitors student's performance and provides tailored resources and activities to maximize their understanding. A student's performance is measured using an AI algorithm and the system adjusts the instruction that they receive accordingly. This approach allows students to experience greater success in their learning as they are engaged in activities that are tailored to their current understanding.

Another way to leverage AI for personalized instruction is through the use of educational bots. Bots can be used to interact with students in the classroom to review completed activities and engage them in activities that further their understanding. Educational bots can also suggest supplemental activities to ensure that students are adequately prepared for future instruction.

Data-driven analytics are also an effective tool in leveraging AI for personalized instruction. By using data analytics, teachers can evaluate a student's understanding and proactively recommend tailored learning activities to better support their comprehension. Data-driven analytics are invaluable to maximize learning outcomes as they allow more targeted instruction to ensure that students are progressing within the course material.

For AI to improve learning outcomes in the classroom, it is essential for teachers to understand the capabilities of the technology and the strategies that can be employed to utilize it. Implementing AI into the classroom should involve developing an individualized learning plan that caters to the student's progress. AI technology can be leveraged to support ongoing development of topics to keep students engaged and ensure they stay on track. Additionally, AI should be used in combination with interactive activities that encourage active learning to further maximize positive outcomes.

AI can be an effective tool to use in the classroom to personalize instruction and maximize learning outcomes. AI technology and algorithms can be used to tailor an individual's learning experience by evaluating their performance and progress. Incorporating personalization strategies such as adaptive learning, educational bots, and data-driven analytics can enable teachers to more closely monitor student success and ensure they receive much-needed support to progress within their course.

Chapter 3: "Unlocking the Potential of AI-Powered Personalized Learning Strategies for the Classroom."

The use of artificial intelligence (AI) in education is becoming increasingly popular as educational institutions strive to leverage modern technologies to enhance teaching and learning. AI-powered personalized learning strategies offer the potential to create an optimal learning experience, providing students with personalized instruction to better meet their individual needs. This technology can help to create a more inclusive learning environment, as well as facilitate improved learning outcomes for all students.

Personalized learning strategies using AI technology use data to provide customized instruction and resources for individual students. AI algorithms track various aspects of a student's progress, from time spent on tasks to answers given on assessments. This data is then used to tailor reading materials, lesson plans, and assignment instructions to the individual needs of each student. By providing tailored engagement, AI technology can create an individualized learning journey that is designed to meet the needs and abilities of each student.

In addition to supporting personalized instructional delivery, AI-powered personalized learning strategies offer a range of other benefits in the classroom. For instance, AI can be used to provide targeted, real-time feedback to drive learning and inform instruction. AI also has the potential to provide learners with personalized and tailored assignments, helping to ensure that students stay engaged and motivated in their learning. Furthermore, AI is being used to facilitate progress tracking and assessment, to both measure student understanding and identify personalized support needs.

The potential of AI-powered personalized learning strategies is exciting and far-reaching. However, to effectively use this technology, educational institutions must have the right infrastructure and expertise in place. In particular, it is essential that institutions have the appropriate technical infrastructure to enable the systems to operate effectively. This infrastructure includes robust data and analytics capabilities, such as the ability to gather, store, and process data. Additionally, appropriate tools must also be in place to manage, support, and guide the personalized learning process.

For technical requirements, educational institutions must also consider the human element when using AI-powered personalized learning strategies. To ensure the technology is implemented effectively, teachers must have the right training and expertise to work with the systems and interpret the data. In addition, educators must be supported when challenging students and pushing further boundaries of learning. Finally, they must also be able to use the results of AI applications to shape instruction and provide frequent, timely feedback to all students.

By understanding and addressing the key challenges associated with the implementation of AI-powered personalized learning strategies, educational institutions can unlock the potential of these strategies to improve teaching and learning in the classroom. To do so, institutions should ensure that they have the right infrastructure and expertise in place, including robust data and analytics capabilities and appropriate tools for managing and guiding the personalized learning process. Educators must be suitably trained and supported to ensure the successful implementation of the technology. When these challenges are addressed, educational institutions can create an optimal learning experience that will benefit all students.

Chapter 4: "Maximizing Learning Potential with AI-Powered Personalized Strategies in the Classroom."

As more advancements are made in the arena of AI-powered learning, the opportunity to maximize learning potential within the classroom is growing significantly. AI-powered personalization provides the foundation upon which educators and learners can take full advantage of these advances in order to optimize their learning experiences. Through the use of intelligent automation, content adaptation, and personalized guidance, AI-powered personalized strategies can help learners gain access to the best learning outcomes and ultimately maximize their learning potential within the classroom.

AI-Powered Intelligent Automation

AI-powered intelligent automation can be used to help learners and teachers manage their daily activities and tasks. By taking into account the current needs and preferences of learners and educators, AI-powered intelligent automation can automate the most time-consuming activities such as grading, lesson planning, and feedback. This allows learners and teachers alike to focus more of their efforts and energy on tasks that are designed to maximize learning potential. Furthermore, AI-powered intelligent automation can also help teachers to quickly identify areas of improvement for learners and provide timely feedback.

Content Adaptation

Through content adaptation, AI-powered personalized strategies are used to match the appropriate level of content to the learner's current abilities and interests. By tailoring the material to the individual learner's needs, it can be easier to maintain learners' attention and interest in the material. As material has the ability to be more tailored to the individual, the level of engagement in the material can increase, leading to learning retention and comprehension. Additionally, the level of content can be adjusted both manually and automatically, making it easier for teachers to identify if instructional content requires recalibration.

Personalized Guidance

One of the strongest benefits of AI-powered personalized strategies is the ability to provide personalized guidance to each learner. By utilizing data collected from learners during the course of their educational journey, AI-powered personalized guidance can help learners take steps towards reaching their educational goals. Furthermore, personalized guidance can also help teachers to better understand each learner's learning capabilities and difficulties, allowing them to make more informed decisions regarding their instructional plans and activities. Intelligent algorithms are also being developed which can analyze large data sets in order to identify areas for improvement in each learner's on the whole learning trajectory.

Maximize Learning Potential

To maximize learning potential within the modern classroom, the use of AI-powered personalized strategies is becoming increasingly important. By utilizing intelligent automation, content adaptation, and personalized guidance, educators and learners alike can take full advantage of these advances in order to optimize their learning experiences. Not only can this enable learner performance to excel, but it also means that student engagement with the material can increase, leading to thorough comprehension and retention of the knowledge and skills learned within the classroom.

Chapter 5: "Harnessing the Power of AI to Create Personalized Learning Experiences in the Classroom".

AI or artificial intelligence is quickly becoming a powerful tool for educators seeking to create more personalized learning experiences within the classroom. It has been shown to significantly increase student engagement and understanding, while allowing teachers to focus on individual learning needs and personalize the learning experience for every student. Additionally, AI can be used to create dynamic learning environments that engage students and enhance their learning experiences.

One of the primary ways in which AI can be used to create more personalized learning experiences in the classroom is through adaptive learning. Adaptive learning refers to computer programs that are designed to personalize instruction and assessment based on a student's unique needs. These AI-powered programs can assess a student's current understanding of a subject in order to provide tailored instruction and assessments that are designed to move the student forward. Additionally, adaptive learning programs can monitor student progress and provide timely feedback to keep students engaged. By utilizing AI-enabled adaptive learning programs, teachers can create more personalized learning experiences tailored to each student's individual needs.

Another way AI can be leveraged to create personalized learning experiences in the classroom is through natural language processing. Natural language processing is a type of AI technology that involves analyzing and understanding written or spoken language. NLP can be used to create AI-based chatbots that facilitate student communication. Chatbots can provide students with personalized feedback, advice, and support as they work through their course materials. Furthermore, chatbots can be programmed to provide students with specific information pertaining to their subject or topic. By leveraging NLP through AI-based chatbots, teachers can create more authentic and personalized learning experiences that enhance student comprehension and engagement.

A third way AI can be used to create personal learning experiences in the classroom is by using AI to facilitate self-directed learning. Self-directed learning refers to a student's ability to take control of their own education through exploration and independent study. AI can be leveraged to provide students with personalized recommendations for which materials to explore based on their current level of understanding and interests. Additionally, AI-driven applications can be used to track student progress and provide data-driven feedback to ensure students are on the right track and to motivate them to explore new topics. By utilizing AI to create modern self-directed learning experiences, teachers can create more personalized learning experiences that support student autonomy and give their students the confidence to explore and excel.

AI can be utilized to create personalized learning experiences through predictive analytics. Predictive analytics is an AI powered technology that utilizes data to analyze student behavior and tailor learning experiences to accommodate individual needs. Predictive analytics can be used to identify learning patterns and behaviors and provide educators with insight into how to better meet the needs of their students. Predictive analytics can be used to monitor student engagement and suggest personalized learning strategies and objectives tailored to the individual. By utilizing predictive analytics, teachers can provide their students with more personalized learning experiences that are tailored to their individual needs and goals.

AI is quickly becoming a powerful tool for educators seeking to create more personalized learning experiences within the classroom. By leveraging AI-powered adaptive learning programs, natural language processing, self-directed learning experiences, and predictive analytics, teachers can provide their students with tailored learning experiences that are designed to maximize student engagement and comprehension. Through the use of AI, teachers can create modern learning environments that foster student growth and provide personalized learning experiences for every student in the classroom.

Chapter 6: "Unlocking the Potential of AI-Powered Personalized Learning in the Classroom"

The potential of AI-powered personalized learning in the classroom is immense, and it has the potential to revolutionize the way students learn in the classroom. While AI technology has become increasingly prevalent in modern society—from smartphones and fitness trackers to automobiles—integrating artificial intelligence into the classroom can yield amazing benefits for students, teachers, and parents alike. By utilizing machine learning and natural language processing, AI-powered personalized learning is able to create individualized learning plans for students that are informed by data from previous assessments, cross-curricular research, and real-time student feedback.

Through its ability to provide dynamic feedback and course adjustment in real time, AI-powered personalized learning can help students learn more effectively, gain a better understanding and mastery of subject material, and in turn reach their educational goals much faster than traditional learning methods can provide. Additionally, AI-powered learning can provide unparalleled accuracy in tracking and analysis of educational data, helping teachers to better understand a student's strengths, weaknesses, and learning preferences, allowing for tailored, individualized instruction.

AI-powered personalized learning can also enable students to customize their own learning paths by allowing them to pick and choose topics from their course, set learning goals, and even take part in virtual laboratories and online tutorials. By providing students with a sense of control and ownership over their education, AI-powered learning will encourage them to take an active role in their education and become more interested in the topics they are studying. With the help of AI-driven learning, teachers can also adjust course content to match students' performance, provide personalized feedback in different ways, and help students stay focused while mastering the content that is most important to them.

Communication between students and teachers can also be improved with AI-powered personalized learning. Through AI-assisted algorithms, conversations between teachers and students can be tailored to each student's learning style, helping to promote real-time feedback and more meaningful conversations. In addition, AI-driven personalization can help teachers more efficiently monitor student progress, prioritize student needs, and provide tailored feedback that can be applied to future lessons.

Ultimately, AI-powered personalized learning provides a unique way to customize instruction and promote student success in the classroom. With its ability to adapt to a student's learning pace and preferences, AI-driven personalization can help teachers create individualized learning plans based on data-driven evidence. This allows students to be exposed to more tailored instruction that can help them achieve their goals at a much faster rate. As students become more interested and engaged in the learning process, they are able to receive more in-depth instruction and gain a deeper understanding of the topics they are studying. In the end, AI-powered personalized learning has the potential to truly revolutionize the way students learn in the classroom.

Chapter 7: "Leveraging AI to Create Tailored Learning Experiences in the Classroom."

The use of artificial intelligence (AI) in the classroom has been gaining increasing attention among educators. AI has the potential to provide tailored learning experiences that are customized to individual student needs — experiences that are more engaging, efficient and effective for students. AI can help teachers in a variety of ways. It can be used to assess students' abilities, providing detailed data to teachers that can be used to structure lessons and personalize instruction. It can also provide personalized remediation and recommendations for interventions. AI can also be used to generate curricula and resources that are tailored to individual students' needs.

There are a few key ways AI can be used to create tailored learning experiences. The first is by using AI-powered adaptive learning tools that measure student progress and adjust the difficulty of the content accordingly. This provides personalized instruction that delivers increased engagement at the student's individual learning level. AI-powered tools can also be used to create more personalized assessments. For example, AI can be used to tailor the difficulty of test questions or to generate assessments that are customized to individual student strengths and weaknesses. AI can also be used to generate customized instruction for individual students. For example, AI can be used to recommend instructional videos, activities, and other resources that are tailored to a student's current level of understanding.

Regarding AI-powered adaptive learning tools, educators can also use AI to create a more personalized learning environment. AI can be used to generate personalized course content and personalized recommendations for learning activities. AI can also be used to provide timely feedback on how well students are grasping the material and can recommend additional material that is most closely related to the student's abilities. AI can also be used to analyze student behavior and interactions in order to create an environment that is more personalized and conducive to learning.

AI can also be used to generate real-time data for use in informing both instructional and behavioral decisions. AI-powered tools can be used to collect data on student performance, as well as student attitudes and interactions in the classroom. This data can be used to inform teachers of where students need additional support, as well as to create an on the whole assessment of the effectiveness of the learning environment.

Artificial intelligence offers tremendous potential for creating tailored classroom learning experiences. AI-powered adaptive learning tools can provide personalized instruction that is tailored to individual student's needs. AI can also be used to create a more personalized learning environment by generating personalized course content, personalized assessments and timely feedback. Finally, AI can be used to collect data on student performance and to inform instructional decisions. By leveraging these tools, educators can create learning experiences that are far more personalized and effective for students.

Chapter 8: "Unlocking the Potential of AI-Powered Personalized Learning in the Classroom"

The potential of AI-powered personalized learning in the classroom is vast and has the potential to revolutionize the educational experience for students in many ways. AI-powered personalized learning can improve the learning experience for students by providing tailored information that is customized to the individual's educational level and needs. This can be done by tracking the student's performance, giving instant feedback, and recommending study materials accordingly. AI-powered personalized learning can also give teachers access to insights about student behavior and performance, enabling them to adjust their lesson plans accordingly for improved learning outcomes.

In order for AI-powered personalized learning to be successful, it has to be used in a manner that is respectful of student privacy, aligns with learning objectives, and takes into consideration the unique needs and learning styles of students. The primary goals of a personalized learning approach should be to provide support and scaffolding for students while helping them to develop the skills and knowledge needed for success in their academic pursuits. First and foremost, the development of a personalized learning environment requires an understanding of the students' varied learning styles and preferences. Consequently, teachers must create activities that are engaging and instructionally relevant; have students identify their learning goals; and ensure that all classroom activities support those goals.

When used strategically, AI-powered personalized learning can enable teachers to manage instructional modules efficiently and effectively, and create personalized learning plans for each student. For example, a teacher could track student progress and performance on assignments, and then arrange instruction according to student needs, or they could use natural language processing to assess student reading levels, and then assign activities accordingly. AI-powered personalized learning can also provide teachers with real-time feedback about student performance, allowing them to quickly identify areas of strength and weakness and adjust their instruction as needed. Finally, AI-powered personalized learning can also reduce the amount of time required to plan instruction, as the AI can be used to create lessons and assign activities that are on target with individual student needs.

When used effectively, AI-powered personalized learning can have significant benefits for students, teachers, and administrators alike. For students, personalized learning can create a more engaging learning environment, as it can produce tailored learning materials that are tailored to their particular learning profile and interests. Teachers can save time and are also able to better identify areas of improvement through real-time data and feedback. Finally, administrators can leverage AI-powered personalized learning to improve on the whole instructional quality, and reduce costs associated with instructional planning.

In order to ensure that AI-powered personalized learning is used effectively in the classroom, it is important to keep the following considerations in mind. Firstly, there needs to be an understanding of the potential risks and implications associated with the use of AI in education, and security measures need to be implemented to protect student data. Secondly, the data models used in the AI technology should be regularly evaluated to ensure that accurate and reliable recommendations are made. Finally, the success of AI-powered personalized learning is critically dependent upon careful monitoring of student progress and feedback.

For AI-powered personalized learning to be successful in the classroom, teachers must be aware of its potential applications and create strategies to maximize its effectiveness. With careful implementation and evaluation, AI-powered personalized learning can revolutionize the learning experience for educators, students, and administrators alike and ensure that all students reach their potential.

Chapter 9: "Harnessing the Power of AI to Create Individualized Learning Environments in the Classroom"

The modern classroom is a rapidly changing environment as advancements in technology offer educators more tools to create individualized learning experiences for students. Artificial Intelligence (AI) is at the forefront of this innovation, allowing educators to create virtual classrooms with personalized instruction and tailored learning paths.

At the most basic level, AI can create an environment where students are provided with learning content tailored to their needs in a very cost-effective way. AI can be used to analyze student data, such as past test scores, course grades, academic performance, attendance, etc., and automatically direct them towards the appropriate instructional material. It can also monitor their progress and offer personalized feedback and recommendations to help them improve. For example, a virtual tutor could recommend specific resources to improve upon a student's current level, from videos to apps and websites to simulations and games.

The use of AI can also create a more secure learning environment by preventing cheating or plagiarism. AI can be used to detect similarities between student work and note where the student may have borrowed from a further source. This helps prevent cheating and plagiarism as it allows the educator to identify the issue and take corrective action.

As AI technology advances, classroom environments will become increasingly personalized and individualized. AI can detect subtle changes in student behavior and use that data to make individualized decisions. AI powered personalized learning systems can monitor students' behavior to create individualized learning plans, tailor instruction to each student's needs, and provide guidance and support so that all students can reach their full potential. AI can also be used to monitor student engagement, providing the educator with insight into which students might be struggling or not receiving the same level of instruction as others.

At the end of the day, AI is revolutionizing the way educators teach. AI provides educators with a powerful tool to harness the power of technology to create individualized learning experiences for students. AI can personalize learning, create secure learning environments, and detect student behavior to make individualized decisions. AI technology continues to improve at an impressive rate, and in the future, we could see AI powering smart classrooms where each student is provided with their own unique course of instruction.

Chapter 10: "Unlocking the Benefits of AI-Powered Personalized Learning for the Classroom"

The use of artificial intelligence (AI) to personalize learning in the classroom is one of the most promising developments in educational technology. The application of AI to classroom learning has the potential to revolutionize student learning by allowing teachers to tailor instruction to the individual needs of each student. AI-powered personalized learning has the potential to improve student achievement, increase engagement, and reduce teacher workload.

AI-powered personalized learning uses artificial intelligence to understand individual student abilities and preferences, and adjust instruction accordingly. For example, an AI-powered learning system may use a student's prior knowledge and interests to decide which topics should be covered in a lesson or what type of material will help the student best understand the material. AI-powered systems may also use student responses to tailor instruction for each student from one moment to the next.

The benefits of AI-powered personalized learning are numerous. By allowing teachers to customize instruction, AI-powered personalized learning can help reduce the amount of time needed to teach a lesson and can result in faster learning outcomes for students. Furthermore, because AI-powered personalized learning eliminates the need to teach a single learning strategy to an entire class of students, it can allow for more personalized instruction and facilitate collaboration among students.

Personalized learning can help reduce distractions in the classroom. AI-powered personalized learning can be used to monitor student attention and progress, and teachers can use this information to identify and address any potential issues related to student engagement. This can reduce distractions from student behaviors that may negatively affect the learning environment.

AI-powered personalized learning can also increase motivation and engagement for students by providing personalized feedback and support. With AI-powered personalized learning, teachers can provide specific, individualized guidance that can help support and motivate students to stay motivated and engaged. This can help students stay on track and gain a greater understanding of the material.

AI-powered personalized learning can reduce teacher workloads by lightening the burden of lesson planning. AI-powered solutions can help teachers create tailored learning activities more quickly by automating parts of the process. This can save teachers time, allowing them to focus more on teaching and interacting with their students.

AI-powered personalized learning has the potential to revolutionize classroom learning. By allowing teachers to tailor instruction to the individual needs of each student, AI-powered personalized learning can improve student achievement, increase motivation and engagement, and reduce teacher workload. As educators embrace the potential of AI-powered personalized learning, teachers can unlock the full potential of personalized instruction and student collaboration.

Chapter 11: "Unlocking the Potential of AI-Powered Personalized Learning in the Classroom"

The education industry is undergoing a digital transformation with the advent of Artificial Intelligence (AI). AI-powered personalized learning in the classroom offers the potential to revolutionize teaching and learning. With traditional learning methods, success depends on how well students learn general concepts taught by teachers. However, personalized learning methods leverage data-driven insights to tailor teaching to the individual needs of each student, enabling them to reach their full potential in the academic setting.

AI-powered personalized learning is an especially effective tool for educators. AI helps teachers to identify each student's unique needs, as well as track progress, tailor instruction, and design personalized learning paths to ensure each student's success. By harnessing the power of AI and data-driven insights, teachers can better understand how each student learns and responds to their individual needs.

AI-powered personalized learning also offers unique opportunities for students. For example, AI can help identify areas where individual students are struggling, create tailored lesson plans to support them, and focus on different types of content to help students better understand complex topics. For example, in multi-age group classes, AI-powered personalized learning can provide differentiated instruction to ensure each individual student is receiving the right level of challenge. Additionally, AI can adjust lessons and educational content to help each student reach their full potential.

Personalized learning extends beyond the classroom and into students' homes. With AI-powered digital learning tools, students can access personalized content according to their individual interests and learning needs. Digital tools can help students practice and reinforce concepts learned in the classroom, enabling them to continue practicing and mastering material outside the traditional classroom setting.

AI-powered personalized learning also offers unique opportunities for administrators. By leveraging data-driven insights, school administrators have the ability to track student progress and help identify any potential areas of improvement. This data-driven approach can help school leaders and educators better understand the needs of their students and provide targeted interventions to ensure students are succeeding at their maximum potential.

AI-powered personalized learning has the potential to revolutionize the education industry, offering unique opportunities for teachers, students, and administrators alike. Not only will this approach help individualize instruction and support students' learning needs, but it can also empower administrators to track progress and better understand the needs and challenges of their student body. By leveraging AI-powered personalization, teachers, students, and administrators can unlock the potential of their academic institutions and unlock a new level of success.

Chapter 12: "Unlocking Student Potential with AI-Powered Personalized Learning Strategies."

The use of Artificial Intelligence (AI) - powered personalized learning strategies is allowing educators to unlock and maximize the potential of students in all areas of learning. By using AI-based technologies and personalized learning algorithms to provide individualized instruction, educators are able to customize learning experiences so that students can achieve their highest levels of success. This article will discuss the various ways in which AI-powered personalized learning strategies can empower teachers and students in the classroom.

One of the primary goals of AI-powered personalized learning strategies is to improve student outcomes through adaptive learning. Adaptive learning utilizes AI to assess a student's individual abilities and adjust the lesson plans accordingly. For instance, if a student is struggling with a particular concept, AI will provide the educator with additional resources or explanatory videos to better explain the concept. This enables students to acquire information they may have otherwise been unable to absorb. As a result, the number of students advancing to higher levels of understanding increases, resulting in better on the whole student outcomes.

Another advantage of using AI-powered personalized learning strategies is that they can help teachers identify students who may be struggling with certain concepts or topics. Using AI algorithms, teachers can analyze data regarding how students are responding to lessons and adjust them accordingly. This can help teachers tailor activities and instruction to the needs of each individual student, providing them with the resources and guidance they need to move their learning forward. As a result, students are able to acquire the knowledge and skills more quickly and effectively, and their performance increases.

AI-mediated personalized learning strategies can also be used to improve communication between students and teachers. For instance, AI-enabled platforms can be used to create virtual classrooms in which students and teachers can engage in interactive conversations. In these conversations, students can ask questions, get feedback from teachers, and receive personalized guidance. In addition, AI-powered platforms can analyze data from the conversations, providing teachers with valuable information about student learning behavior and progress.

AI-powered personalized learning strategies can be used to create engaging learning materials and activities. Using AI-based technologies, educators can create activities that are personalized to the interests and capabilities of each student. This helps keep students engaged and motivated to continue learning, which leads to better on the whole student outcomes.

AI-powered personalized learning strategies are allowing educators to empower students by providing them with personalized learning experiences. These strategies are helping teachers identify students who need additional resources and guidance. They are also helping students achieve better outcomes by personalizing instruction to their individual learning needs. Finally, AI-enabled platforms are providing students with engaging learning materials and activities. By implementing these strategies, educators are able to unlock the full potential of their students while helping them achieve their highest levels of success.

Chapter 13: "Leveraging AI to Enhance Personalized Learning In the Classroom".

As technology is rapidly evolving, it has become necessary for educators to explore new strategies to educate their students. Artificial Intelligence (AI) has the potential to revolutionize the way we think about teaching and learning. AI can offer an unprecedented degree of flexibility and customization when it comes to personalized learning.

Personalized learning allows students to receive an education tailored to their individual needs and preferences. Instead of having everyone learn the same material at the same pace, personalized learning allows students to progress at their own speed and develop skills and knowledge according to their own capabilities. By leveraging AI, educators can more easily and accurately identify each student's unique needs and deliver customized instruction.

AI can be used in the classroom to provide teachers with insights into each student's strengths, weaknesses, interests, and learning styles. This can be done through the use of AI-enabled devices such as tablets and laptops, which can collect data on individual student performance. By analyzing this data, teachers can better understand their students and provide each learner with the best possible learning experience.

AI can also be used to create and deliver personalized learning experiences based on the individual learner's characteristics. There are a variety of AI-based applications that can be used to create dynamic learning activities based on a student's prior knowledge and interests. AI can also automate the assessment process, which can help teachers quickly understand how their students are progressing and identify areas of improvement.

By implementing AI-powered personalized learning, AI can also be used to develop more interactive and engaging educational experiences. AI-based tools can be used to create interactive learning environments and adaptive learning scenarios. For example, AI chatbots can offer conversational tutoring, allowing students to ask questions, receive feedback, and work through problems in real-time.

AI-powered platforms, such as virtual and augmented reality, can also create highly engaging educational environments. AI can also be used to develop learning games and simulations that can help students better understand concepts in a more engaging and memorable way.

AI can be used to automate processes and improve workflow management. AI-based applications can be used to streamline grading, lesson planning, and classroom communication. This can help teachers save time and allow them to focus more on providing personalized instruction.

AI has the potential to revolutionize the way we think about teaching and learning. By leveraging AI to deliver personalized instruction, teachers can better engage their students, meet the needs of each student, and provide a more enjoyable and effective educational experience. AI can also be used to create innovative learning strategies, analyze student performance, and automate administrative tasks. By taking advantage of these advantages, teachers can ensure their students receive the best possible education.

Chapter 14: "Leveraging AI for Personalized Learning: Strategies for the Classroom".

The potential of artificial intelligence (AI) to transform education is just beginning to be realized. AI has the ability to provide personalized, adaptive learning experiences for students based on their individual needs and interests. This could enable educators to create more effective learning experiences while allowing for greater student engagement and retention. In the classroom, AI can be used in a number of ways to create a more personalized learning experience for students.

One of the most common ways to utilize AI in the classroom is through the use of adaptive learning systems. These systems use AI to provide students with personalized feedback based on their individual learning needs and goals. Adaptive learning systems can be used to analyze student performance data and generate individualized guidance for students based on their unique strengths and weaknesses. This type of system can be especially beneficial for students who may be struggling in a particular area or subject, as it can provide them with tailored support and guidance.

Another way to use AI in the classroom is through the use of natural language processing (NLP). NLP is the process by which machines can understand human language, and it can be used to create personalized learning experiences for students. For example, NLP-based systems can analyze text-based conversations between a student and teacher and identify areas of difficulty or confusion for the student. This allows the teacher to provide the student with more targeted support and resources to address these issues and ensure they are getting the most out of their learning experience.

AI can also be used to optimize teachers' workflow. AI-driven tools can analyze data from student assessments, analyze the results, and provide feedback to the teacher on how to improve instruction. AI-based tools can also be used to create lesson plans automatically, allowing teachers to spend more time engaging with their students and providing individualized guidance.

AI can be utilized for personalized learning through the use of virtual reality (VR). VR can be used to create immersive learning environments that are tailored to the individual student's interests and learning styles. This type of technology can be used to create virtual classrooms, allowing students to explore topics and engage with subjects in more meaningful ways. Virtual reality can also be used to simulate real-world scenarios, providing students with a hands-on learning experience.

As AI technology continues to advance, there are an increasing number of ways that educators can incorporate it into the classroom to create a more personalized learning experience for their students. From adaptive learning systems to virtual reality, AI has the potential to revolutionize the way that students learn, allowing educators to provide targeted, engaging instruction tailored to each student's individual needs and interests. The future of personalized learning will be one that is driven by artificial intelligence and educators should begin to explore how they can leverage AI in the classroom to create more effective learning experiences for their students.

Chapter 15: "Unlocking the Potential of AI-Powered Personalized Learning in the Classroom."

The potential of Artificial Intelligence (AI)-powered personalized learning has been increasingly acknowledged in the classroom by educators as a way to improve student engagement and on the whole performance. This technology has the potential to revolutionize existing teaching methods by enabling teachers to deliver tailored content to meet individual students' needs and interests; unleashing the full potential of AI-powered personalized learning therefore lies in its ability to empower educators to address the wide variety of student learning styles, needs, and interests as well as truly respond to any valid concern for any given student.

The concept of personalized learning is actually impossible to achieve without the use of AI-powered technology, which is why many are now turning to such solutions to further empower teaching and learning initiatives, especially in this era of enhanced digital transformation. AI-powered personalization offers a variety of advantages for both educators and students.

For teachers, the ability to customize each individual student's learning journey is a huge bonus. By providing students with access to a variety of learning resources, teachers can ensure that each student's specific learning objectives are being met. For example, AI-powered personalized learning can cater to the various skill levels of every learner, allowing teachers to adjust instruction, practice questions, and resources to best suit their students. This type of learning can also provide teachers with the flexibility to respond to changing student needs and interests in real-time, giving them the opportunity to more effectively support their students' learning.

For students, AI-powered personalized learning has the power to engage learners more than ever before. Through targeted content and personalized assessments, students can easily identify what areas they need to improve and focus on accordingly. The emphasis on student choice and autonomy can also help build student confidence, knowing that the subject material is tailored to each individual.

One of the primary goals of personalized learning in the classroom is to create richer learning experiences for all students. With AI-powered technologies, teachers can strive to differentiate instruction and to create learning pathways tailored to the specific preferences and needs of each student. By individualizing the learning journey for each student, students have more opportunities to engage, explore, and develop meaningful learning experiences.

The potential of AI-powered personalized learning is clear in its ability to empower educators and enhance student engagement. With personalized learning tailored specifically to each student, the learning experience is richer, and students can become more confident and motivated to reach their potential. AI-powered personalized learning has the potential to revolutionize teaching and learning in the classroom, and educators should be eager to take advantage of it.

Chapter 16: "Leveraging AI to Create Personalized Learning Experiences in the Classroom"

The term artificial intelligence (AI) has been increasingly gaining traction over the last couple of years. AI is increasingly seen as a way to provide personalized learning experiences in the classroom. AI is essentially a computer program that can learn from data and make decisions, making it suitable for personalized education.

Personalized learning experiences are designed to tailor content to individual student needs. This means that teachers can create individual lesson plans and resources for each student to target their strengths and weaknesses. Thus, teaching can be more efficient and effective, and students can be motivated to learn.

AI can enable personalized learning experiences by providing insights into individual students based on their preferences, abilities and background. For instance, an AI-driven dashboard can provide teachers with a snapshot of each student's performances, including which topics they are doing well or struggling in. With this data, the teacher can quickly assess the progress of each student and adjust their teaching style accordingly.

Teachers can also leverage AI-driven technologies to create dynamic lessons that adapt to each student's needs. For instance, AI-driven assessments can be used to measure each student's understanding of different topics. The AI can assess the results and recommend additional learning materials or activities based on each student's individual performance. This will ensure that each student receives the instruction that is tailored to their abilities and needs.

Another way AI can enable personalized learning experiences is through personalized content delivery. AI-driven programs can help teachers design lessons that reach each student on a personal level by mining data about the student's interests and preferences. For example, AI could suggest different content such as e-books, videos, articles, and games based on the student's past performance or interests.

AI can be used to create personalized student assessments. AI-driven assessments can assess each student's understanding of the material in detail and provide suggestions to further enhance their learning. AI can recognize individual student's strengths and weaknesses and adjust the curriculum accordingly, allowing the teacher to focus on the topics that each student needs the most help in.

AI can be used to provide personalized feedback and grading for each student. AI-driven programs can quickly assess the student's work and provide immediate feedback. This feedback can give the teacher more time to provide additional support to students who need it the most.

AI is a tool that can be used to create personalized learning experiences in the classroom. It can provide teachers with insights into individual student strengths and weaknesses, help them create dynamic lessons, and suggest personalized content for different students. AI can also create personalized assessments and provide quick feedback and grading for each student. These advantages make AI a powerful tool for creating enjoyable learning experiences in the classroom.

Chapter 17: "Harnessing the Power of AI to Optimize Personalized Learning Experiences in the Classroom."

The use of Artificial Intelligence (AI) in classrooms across the globe is quickly becoming a reality. As more schools embrace its power, the potential of AI to optimize personalized learning experiences in the classroom is becoming increasingly evident. Utilizing AI in the classroom presents a unique opportunity for teachers to provide tailored learning experiences to each student in their class, leading to more efficient and effective instruction, improved grades, enhanced creativity and exploration, and increased engagement.

To begin, AI can be used to create a personalized learning environment for each student. AI tools are able to analyze a student's data, such as their individual learning style, prior knowledge, academic performance, and interests, to construct an individualized "learning path" aimed to best meet their needs. Through this customized approach, teachers are able to deliver customized instruction to each student and focus on their specific weaknesses and strengths, allowing them to direct their energy as efficiently as possible. Additionally, AI-generated curriculum can generate various instructional strategies, activities, and assignments to help students achieve desired learning goals.

By providing a personalized learning environment, AI can also assist teachers in better assessing student learning. Utilizing AI-based software, teachers can identify which areas each student needs to focus on in order to make the greatest gains. AI also provides teachers with important analytics to review student performance, track progress, and measure outcomes. This helps teachers understand which strategies are working and which need to be adjusted, as well as identify any learning challenges or gaps quickly and accurately, so they can adapt the curriculum appropriately. These insights also help teachers provide better support and guidance to each student and help them make informed decisions about how best to measure and assess learning progress.

AI can be used to create engaging and interactive learning experiences for students. AI-driven content can be tailored to each student's individual needs and interests, providing greater engagement and motivation in the classroom. Additionally, AI can create interactive simulations, games, and virtual reality experiences to support the learning process, providing students with an engaging and entertaining way to learn. This highly personalized, technology-driven learning environment can be a motivating factor for students and help them stay engaged.

Harnessing the power of AI to optimize personalized learning experiences in the classroom is essential to supporting and motivating students, and improving educational outcomes. AI provides teachers with an opportunity to create an effective, individualized learning environment that is engaging for students and can lead to more effective instruction and higher educational outcomes. As the use of AI continues to evolve, the potential for schools to further optimize student learning experiences also continues to grow.

Chapter 18: "Harnessing the Power of AI to Enhance Personalized Learning in the Classroom".

A considerable amount of attention has recently been given to the power of artificial intelligence (AI) to enhance personalized learning in the classroom. For educators, the potential of AI in personalizing curriculum has been a major focus for the past few years. While there is still much to be discovered in terms of the practical application of AI in personalizing education, evidence is beginning to emerge that suggest the use of AI can result in improved learning outcomes amongst students and a more rewarding experience for both learners and educators. In this chapter, we will discuss the power of AI to enable personalized learning in the classroom, the various applications of AI, and suggestions of practical ways educators and institutions can begin to harness the power of AI for enhanced educational delivery.

It is important to understand the value of personalized learning in the classroom setting. Personalized learning, when done right, meets each learner's unique needs, interests, and goals. Students are able to absorb information more easily when it is tailored to their individual needs. Personalized learning also helps make students more self-reliant and encourages them to develop their own decision-making processes, critical thinking, and problem-solving skills.

The rise of artificial intelligence has made it a powerful tool for use in personalized learning. AI can be used to tailor learning material to the individual needs of each learner. AI can be used to detect and analyze specific patterns which can then be used to personalize the learning experience for each specific student. For example, AI can be used to monitor student engagement levels, track student progress, and identify areas of difficulty for individual students

Chapter 19: "Leveraging AI for Personalized Classroom Learning Experiences."

The effective integration of artificial intelligence (AI) into existing classroom learning experiences calls for its application in a manner that accounts for the individual needs of students, and also provides meaningful, personalized instruction. Implementing AI effectively into the classroom is beneficial to students, parents, and educators alike, as it enables the use of adaptive learning models that can be customized to each student's particular learning needs. AI can even be used to assess the progress of individual students to ensure they stay on track with classroom objectives. In this manner, AI can be leveraged to provide a more customized learning experience for each student, leading to improved performance and increased engagement.

To start, AI can be used to create adaptive learning systems that can recognize a student's unique learning needs and provide an individualized learning experience. This process begins with the development of an AI-powered analytics platform that can analyze individual learning data, such as student performance data and usage activity data. Such intelligence-driven solutions can then be harnessed to create personalized learning models that can adapt in real-time to student behavior and adjust the instruction content accordingly. By doing this, educators can ensure that students receive content that is more tailored to their specific learning needs and thereby enable students to achieve better outcomes.

AI-driven classroom tools can be used to monitor student performance and deliver feedback in a personalized manner. For example, AI-driven instruction tools can be programmed to provide personalized feedback to students that is tailored to their performance and interests. This enables teachers to adjust the instruction material to the student's ability level and provide real-time guidance and mentorship. Such AI-driven feedback also enables the educator to provide direct and timely feedback that can be taken into account by the student to improve their performance.

Another benefit that can be realized by leveraging AI for personalized learning experiences is its ability to facilitate collaboration and communication between students and educators. AI-enabled tools enable teachers to monitor student performance, foster a learning community within the classroom, and facilitate conversation between students. Furthermore, AI-driven classrooms also allow students to interact with their peers to pose questions, share information, and discuss lessons. Such meaningful interactions enable students to stay on track with their course objectives in a highly engaging manner.

AI can be leveraged to create customized learning assessments that measure a student's progress. For example, AI-powered algorithms can be used to administer tests that target a student's specific learning needs and mimic a real-world learning experience. This enables educators to identify learning gaps and provide more feedback on individual performance. Furthermore, AI-powered assessments can serve as a proactive measure, as they can help teachers identify potential quiet achievers more quickly and recognize when a student may be struggling and in need of additional guidance.

The implications of leveraging AI for personalized classroom learning experiences are wide-reaching and highly beneficial. AI-enabled instructional tools and assessments not only provide meaningful, personalized instruction for each student, but also enable educators to deliver real-time feedback and closely monitor the progress of their students. This helps to ensure that each student's progress is optimally monitored and instruction is tailored to their individual learning needs – all of which enhances the learning experience and results in improved performance.

Chapter 20: "Leveraging AI for Enhanced Personalization in the Classroom: Strategies for Optimized Learning."

Personalization is the key to successful learning. Despite the large amount of data available and the ever-evolving technologies such as Artificial Intelligence (AI), customization in learning has not been explored completely and continues to be a challenge. AI helps to bridge this gap, allowing teachers to customize the curriculum and activities for each student, making the most of their potential. AI enables teachers to better understand, monitor and predict students' needs and interests, enabling them to deliver the most appropriate learning experience.

As Artificial Intelligence is growing in popularity, educators and students are increasingly asking what AI-driven personalized learning can do for them. Personalized learning is a process whereby the teacher tailors the content and learning activities to the individual student. It can include personalization of content, activities, assessments, and learning activities; differentiated instructions; and a focus on personalized feedback. AI can bring personalized learning to life, as it can analyze large and complex data sets to identify patterns, detect anomalies and enable individualized instruction. This new technology offers enormous opportunities to tailor learning to the needs of each student, leading to improved academic performance and better outcomes for all.

There are various strategies for leveraging AI to enhance personalization in the classroom. First, teachers must have access to data tracking and analytics functions that can be used to measure, analyze, and compare student performance, enabling them to make better-informed decisions. Second, AI can be used to customize course content and activities to the individual student, providing timely and relevant content. Third, AI-driven assessment and testing tools can be used to identify students' strengths, weaknesses and their on the whole learning capacity. Finally, AI can be used to provide personalized feedback to students, helping them develop targeted learning strategies and improving focus.

To further improve personalization, teachers should keep track of individual student information, such as interests, learning styles, and individual goals. This data can help teachers develop personalized learning plans for each student. Additionally, AI can be used to connect students with peers who have similar learning interests, allowing them to learn together by engaging in collaborative activities and discussions.

The potential of AI is immense, and it can lead to an optimized and personalized learning experience. It is essential that teachers understand the potential of the technology and use it effectively for the greatest benefit of their students. AI can enable more efficient and accurate assessment, allow educators to create personalized learning plans for every student, and facilitate more effective communication between teachers and students. AI technology can save time and cost, while delivering more personalized instruction, leading to improved student performance and better on the whole outcomes. It is important that educators understand the importance of leveraging AI technology in the classroom and use it to assure the best possible learning experience for all.

Chapter 21: "Unlocking the Power of AI for Personalized Learning in the Classroom"

The potential of Artificial Intelligence (AI) to revolutionize education is both intriguing and exciting. AI is becoming increasingly important as a tool in many areas, from marketing to healthcare. There is also potential for it to transform the education sector, and more specifically, personalized learning in the classroom.

Personalized learning is an approach used in many classrooms to better meet students' individual needs and optimize their learning experience. Through this method, each student has their own unique, tailored educational plan that focuses on their individual strengths, weaknesses, interests, and abilities. The implementation of AI in personalized learning could provide unprecedented opportunities for students to reach their educational goals.

To begin with, AI can be used to customize learning material and activities for each student at an individual level, based on their interests and needs. This means lessons can become individually tailored towards their experience, skills, and abilities, which could increase their engagement and motivation to learn. AI also has the capability to gather data on appropriate learning times and experiences for each student to maximize their attention span and further improve their learning experience.

AI can help teachers create personalized learning activities for each student based on their progress in the course. This would help teachers identify any weak areas that need more focus and attention. AI technology can also be used to gather data on how individual students respond to particular activities and lesson styles, allowing a teacher the ability to adjust the approach taken to improve their results.

Furthermore, AI has the potential to improve communication and collaboration between teachers and students. AI-powered chatbots can be used to answer students' questions in real-time and to respond to any queries they may have relating to their studies. This would be beneficial to both teachers and students, as teachers would be able to devote more of their time to providing one-on-one assistance and feedback to their students, while students would be able to get answers to their questions while they are still studying.

Perhaps one of the most exciting potentials of AI in personalized learning is to identify patterns in students' learning experience, allowing teachers to better understand their objectives and adjust their approach accordingly. This could also be beneficial to foster a more personal environment and learning experience, where students are encouraged to ask questions and receive real-time feedback on their progress.

Perhaps the most invaluable result of using AI in personalized learning, is its ability to assist with the scalability of its efforts, making it more accessible to different educational contexts. By providing access to personalized learning experiences, AI can offer learners an opportunity to access higher quality education and the scaling of such systems is clearly desirable.

The potential of AI in personalized learning in the classroom is esteemed, and its impact has the potential to revolutionize the education sector. Through this advanced technology, teachers can better understand their students' needs and adjust their approach accordingly, while students will be able to benefit from a tailored and engaging learning experience. Through AI, everyone in the educational system will be able to gain access to higher quality education. As such, the importance of this technology in the classroom is readily apparent and may soon become a key tool in the classroom.

Chapter 22: "Unlocking the Potential of AI for Personalized Learning in the Classroom".

The potential of artificial intelligence (AI) to revolutionize education is growing exponentially. AI-driven personalized learning is transforming how teachers and students engage and interact in the classroom. AI-driven teaching systems are now being used to provide personalized instruction for students of all ages and backgrounds. AI is impacting the educational experience by increasing engagement in content, providing feedback on performance, delivering individualized instruction, and more.

At its core, personalized learning is about creating individualized learning experiences for each student, based on their individual needs. AI-driven personalized learning uses Artificial Intelligence algorithms to respond to individual student performance and customize learning paths accordingly. AI is able to produce personalized learning experiences tailored to the individual student ability or interest level and provide the best possible instruction for them in the fastest and most effective way. Material can be presented in different ways for different students, ultimately creating a learning experience tailored to each of them.

AI can make it easier for teachers to track student progress over time. For instance, AI- enabled systems can provide real-time feedback on student progress. Teachers can use the data to make better-informed decisions about instruction and individual student needs. Furthermore, AI can be used to arrange student groups according to their abilities and preferences, so that lessons can be tailored to the students who make up different groups.

AI also has great potential to support differentiated instruction, where each student receives instruction at their own pace and level of understanding. AI-driven systems can detect individual student patterns and readjust instruction accordingly to ensure the most effective learning. With AI, teachers can monitor progress in real-time and tailor instruction accordingly. AI also has the potential to improve student assessment by providing more accurate and reliable assessment data. With AI, teachers can quickly analyze student performance and gain valuable insights into student needs.

Another use for AI in the classroom is to provide a virtual tutor. AI-driven virtual learning programs can provide personalized instruction through voice and facial recognition, chatbot conversations, and other interactive programs. Students can ask questions to their virtual tutors and receive helpful feedback. AI can also be used to help develop personalized study plans for students. AI can help students set achievable goals and build a plan toward success.

AI has the potential to revolutionize personalized learning by providing personalized content recommendations. AI-driven systems can scan student profiles, levels of interest, and past performance and then recommend content tailored to each student's interests and abilities. Content which is personalized to each student's level of understanding allows students to better engage and learn more quickly.

The potential of AI for personalized learning in the classroom is vast. AI-driven systems enable personalized instruction, facilitate differentiated teaching, provide virtual tutoring, help develop and create study plans, and provide personalized content recommendations. AI-driven systems can also help to track student progress, provide feedback, and facilitate student assessments. By unlocking the potential of AI for personalized learning in the classroom, both teachers and students can benefit from its powerful capabilities.

Chapter 23: "Unlocking Potential Through AI-Powered Personalized Learning Strategies in the Classroom"

Artificial intelligence (AI) is transforming the way that we teach and learn. Through its use of data and sophisticated algorithms, AI can tailor the educational experience to individuals and unlock their potential. AI-powered personalized learning strategies can offer students personalized instruction, provide them with better guidance, and create learning experiences that are more engaging and directed.

Personalized learning is based on the idea that education should focus on the individual student rather than the entire class. It is an approach to learning that recognizes that each student has different learning styles and needs. AI-powered personalized learning strategies enable teachers to customize lessons to individual students, providing content that is tailored to the student's learning needs and abilities. AI can assess student performance data and offer personalized feedback and guidance to help the student progress in their learning.

Personalized learning experiences provide students with engaging and relevant content that keeps them motivated and interested in the topic. Students have access to a library of multimedia, interactive resources to explore and sharpen their knowledge in a meaningful way. These resources can range from videos, audio recordings, and podcasts to gaming platforms, digital simulations, and interactive activities. AI-powered personalized learning strategies can also incorporate adaptive learning technologies such as artificial intelligence-powered tutoring systems and adaptive assessments which actively adjust in response to the student's input and performance.

This approach to learning can help to reduce the learning gap between students of different backgrounds and abilities. AI-powered personalized learning strategies can detect potential learning challenges and provide instruction with the pace, level of difficulty and individual attention that each student needs. Through the use of supportive technologies, such as virtual teachers and virtual assistants, AI can encourage student success and autonomy. It can also identify and foster learning opportunities, based on the individual's interests and preferences.

AI-powered personalized learning strategies also provide teachers with access to important data which can be used to enhance instruction. Data generated from actionable analytics and AI-based insights can be used to track learning progress, detect potential learning difficulties, and customize instruction to an individual student's needs. It also helps inform the educator's decisions about lesson content and the progression of instruction. AI-powered personalized learning strategies can also be used to inform the teacher's decisions on how best to motivate and engage students.

In the current educational climate, AI-powered personalized learning strategies can unlock the potential of learners of all ages and levels of education. It enables us to tailor learning experiences to the individual, creating a more engaging and meaningful learning experience. Furthermore, with AI-driven personalized learning strategies, educators are better equipped to assess and support the learning needs of the individual. AI-powered personalized learning strategies can be applied in a variety of educational settings, providing learners with access to content that is tailored to their abilities and interests.

With personalized learning, we have the potential to offer students individualized instruction, more guidance, and an engaging and directed learning experience. AI-powered personalized learning strategies are revolutionizing the way we teach and learn, providing teachers with data-driven insights and the tools to create a more informed and personalized approach to instruction. By embracing AI-powered personalized learning strategies, educators can unlock the potential of their entire class and create a more equitable and enjoyable educational environment.

Chapter 24: "Harnessing the Power of AI for Personalized Learning in the Classroom"

In recent years, Artificial Intelligence (AI) has emerged as an unprecedented ally in the education sector, providing teachers with opportunities to create uniquely tailored and individualized learning experiences for their students. AI has made leaps and bounds towards transforming education and enabling more personalized learning experiences in the classroom. With the ability to provide customized interactive learning modules, AI has enabled teachers to provide targeted, data-driven instruction tailored to each student's needs. AI-powered applications such as chatbots, apps and algorithms are being used to reduce the workload of teachers while simultaneously increasing engagement and learning productivity in the classroom.

Connected to the internet, AI tools allow for searches to be done quickly and accurately, reducing the time-consuming task of background research for students. Adaptive learning programs have been designed to provide customized, contextualized learning experiences, comparable to one-on-one tutoring at a fraction of the cost. With the ability to adapt the material to each learner's individual learning style and level of understanding, AI-powered tech can provide an ideal personalized instructional experience for students.

AI is an invaluable helping hand for teachers, providing them with additional intelligence and data to better understand their learners and innovative assess their performance. AI-enabled software can conveniently capture and analyze both academic and behavioral data of each student to assess the progress in real-time, enabling diagnoses and interventions when needed. With the ability to recognize a student's personality and learning patterns, AI can provide insights into their educational journey, allowing for enhanced predictive analytics, risk assessment of student's performance, recommendations for coursework, and personalized assessment.

AI-related learning technologies are also assumed to transform classroom activities in various ways. AI can provide students with clickable, video-based lessons that provide feedback and assess their comprehension of the subject. AI-enhanced apps and platforms can offer games and simulations to engage learners in an immersive, captivating learning experience, while providing student-specific data to give instructors a better understanding of their pupils. AI can also be utilized to generate customized practice tests and assignments that cater to the unique level and needs of each individual learner.

AI-powered virtual reality (VR) technology can transform the learning experience for students. VR applications are a step beyond the traditional and mundane method of learning in the classroom by creating an engaging and interactive environment to learn complex concepts in a simpler manner. Additionally, AI tools such as Natural Language Processing and Machine Learning can translate course material in the student's native language, reducing the language barrier and improving comprehension.

As AI continues to evolve and progress, it has the potential to bring about revolutionary changes in the traditional classroom to provide students with a more personal and effective educational experience. AI can enable teachers to give far more comprehensive feedback to their students and empower them to make better instructional decisions based on individual student data. With the ability to recognize the unique needs and capabilities of each student, AI can drastically improve the effectiveness of learning and the whole quality of education for all.

Chapter 25: "Leveraging AI to Enhance Personalized Learning Experiences in the Classroom"

The potential of Artificial Intelligence (AI) to create more personalized learning experiences in the classroom is stirring up excitement among educators and technology experts. AI can enable educators to analyze large sets of data to identify problems and develop solutions that meet individual needs and improve learning outcomes. By leveraging available AI technology, educators can create a more personal environment in the classroom that stimulates students and encourages them to explore their interests and develop their skills and knowledge.

The key to creating a personalized learning experience is the collection and use of data. AI tools can compile data from multiple sources, such as student surveys, test scores, and attendance records, to identify patterns and trends in student performance. These insights into student behavior, preferences, and performance can inform important decisions about how to design curricula and learning activities that are tailored to individual needs and interests. For instance, AI can be used to analyze student performance to identify weak spots in certain topics, allowing teachers to quickly pinpoint individual areas of focus that can improve mastery of the subject. Furthermore, AI can be used to detect problem behaviors and provide early interventions to stop them from occurring.

AI can also streamline the assessment process in the classroom, allowing for more accurate and quickly-ranked assessments of student work. In the process of formal assessment, AI tools can be used to record and analyze student responses, identify key elements of student engagement, and even suggest ways to improve performance. AI-based assessment can also enable personalized feedback that can be tailored to individual learning styles and levels of ability. This feedback can help to motivate and engage students, as they receive information that is directly and specifically related to their learning needs.

The deployment of AI tools can also help to reduce the "one-size-fits-all" approach to teaching, while facilitating personalized learning tailored to the specific needs of each student. AI-driven learning tools, such as intelligent tutors and augmented reality systems, can gather data on students' level of understanding of a subject and provide customized feedback to individual students. This feedback can range from simple nudges promoting effective study habits, to visual aids and external sources of knowledge for further learning. Furthermore, AI tools can help to stimulate the classroom environment with interactive techniques such as digital simulations and role-playing, which can foster more active engagement in learning.

AI-driven experiences and applications can also bridge the gap between physical and digital learning environments, creating hybrid experiences. For instance, AI-driven technologies, such as virtual reality, can be used to immerse students in realistic 3D environments where they can practice and interact with simulated objects and environments. Hybrid approaches using AI-driven technologies can also be used to enrich classic physical experiences, such as field trips, by augmenting them with interactive digital content and activities.

AI can be used to create personalized educational experiences in the classroom that foster engagement, stimulate interaction, and personalize the learning process. AI has the potential to revolutionize the educational landscape, offering specialized, tailored learning experiences that make learning meaningful and effective in a way that has never been experienced before. This, in turn, can help to foster lifelong learning and critical thinking skills in today's students, ensuring that they remain competitive and successful in a rapidly changing world.

Chapter 26: "Leveraging AI to Create Individualized Student Experiences in the Classroom"

Artificial Intelligence (AI) has been a revolutionary force in our society in recent decades. AI technology has been used all across the world to help improve our lives in a multitude of ways. From medical diagnoses to document analysis to helping with traffic control, AI has been an indispensable addition to humanity. With the advent of modern technology and its increasing accessibility to everyday citizens, AI can now be used to help create individualized student experiences in the classroom. By leveraging AI, teachers, professionals, and parents can provide students with tailored experiences that are tailored specifically to their individual needs.

The ability to personalize student experiences in the classroom has been made possible with the introduction of AI. Teachers can now leverage AI to observe student behavior, track student engagement, and even assess their learning styles and preferences. AI is able to collect data using sensors such as voice recognition, facial recognition, motion detection, and other biometric measures.

For instance, AI can identify students in the classroom that need extra help with certain topics and provide personalized assistance toward mastering the subject. AI can also be used to evaluate student progress and identify areas that need improvement, as well as suggest resources and activities that can help the student learn more quickly and effectively. In addition, AI can be used to create individualized learning plans for each student based on their behaviors, strengths, and weaknesses.

AI also plays an important role in tailoring the classroom environment to each student's individual needs. AI can analyze student performance and apply learning models accordingly to create an optimal learning experience. AI-driven simulations and interactive learning activities can help make learning more engaging and help students stay on task. This, in turn, can lead to higher student achievement and better learning outcomes.

AI can also be used to make sure the classroom environment is suitable for individual students. AI can analyze the interactions between students and their teachers to determine if the student is comfortable and is learning in an optimal way. In addition, AI can recognize and respond to student emotional states and understand their moods. This data can be used to adjust the learning environment so that it is more conducive to learning – allowing for better engagement, focus, and participation.

AI can also perform complex analytics and real-time analysis of student data from multiple sources. This data can be used to create personalized curricula and assessments that meet the individual needs and goals of each student. AI-driven analytics can also inform decisions about classroom instruction and teaching strategies. For instance, AI can evaluate student responses to different learning activities and use this data to adjust the course for more efficient and effective learning.

When it comes to leveraging AI to create individualized student experiences in the classroom, the sky's the limit. AI can be used to collect and analyze student data, provide personalized assistance and create individualized learning plans, create interactive and engaging learning activities, track student performance and progress, and optimize the learning environment. The ability to tailor learning experiences to each student's individual needs and abilities is one of the most exciting applications of AI technology. In the future, AI will be the key to creating a personalized learning environment that encourages engagement, focus, and ultimately better outcomes for students of all ages.

Chapter 27: "Maximizing Learning Potential with AI-Powered Personalized Instruction in the Classroom"

In the modern classroom, it is important to maximize learning potential with AI-powered personalized instruction. As an effective and efficient way to provide students with individualized learning experiences, AI-powered personalized instruction can help teachers tailor instruction to the student's individual learning needs. AI's ability to quickly analyze data sets, spot trends and make predictions makes it a valuable tool for teachers as a virtual educator. As educators look to new technological solutions to provide individualized instruction, AI-powered personalized instruction has become a go-to tool for the most effective classroom teachers.

AI-powered personalized instruction is based on computer-driven algorithms which couples student data with machine learning to create individualized instruction for each student based on his or her needs. This AI-driven data can help teachers determine the best instructional path for students based on analysis that covers a wide range of factors such as grades, assessment scores, attendance, social-emotional state, individual student challenges, workflows, classroom dynamics and more. With AI-powered personalized instruction, students can receive tailored instruction that will help them reach their learning goals faster and more efficiently.

Another benefit of AI-powered personalized instruction is that it allows educators to measure student progress in real-time. By using AI to track student engagement, performance, and other factors, teachers can quickly assess which instruction is proving to be effective or to alter instruction accordingly as needed. Additionally, AI-powered personalized instruction makes it easier for teachers to provide timely feedback to their students. With AI, teachers can quickly analyze large datasets and provide meaningful feedback and personalized guidance to students as needed.

AI-powered personalized instruction also helps teachers to quickly identify learning gaps in the classroom. AI can detect trends and patterns in student data and quickly analyze changes in student performance in order to pinpoint any areas where students are struggling. This information can be used to quickly adjust instruction to help close these learning gaps. AI's ability to quickly detect and monitor changes in student performance can help teachers identify when students need extra help and design personalized instruction to help them move forward.

To help students learn quickly and efficiently, AI-powered personalized instruction also plays a role in helping teachers manage their classrooms. AI can be used to facilitate the individualized instruction that teachers will be providing to their students, thus reducing the teacher's workload. AI can also be used to automate a number of tasks that are part of classroom instruction, such as grading, communicating with students, and tracking student progress. This can help relieve some burden on teachers and the school system, while still providing students with the personalized instruction they need.

AI-powered personalized instruction is an effective tool that can help teachers maximize learning potential in their classrooms. AI's ability to quickly analyze student data and provide personalized instruction allows teachers to design lessons that are tailored to each student's individual needs. AI-powered personalized instruction can also help teachers to identify learning gaps, provide timely feedback, and manage their classrooms more effectively. As technology advances, AI-powered personalized instruction will become an essential tool to help maximize learning potential in the modern classroom.

Chapter 28: "Leveraging AI-Powered Strategies For A More Personalized Classroom Experience"

Artificial intelligence (AI) technology is a rapidly growing force in the educational technology industry. It has the potential to revolutionize the way educators teach and students learn within the classroom. With AI-powered strategies, classrooms can be transformed to provide more personalized learning experiences.

AI-powered strategies for the classroom focus on leveraging predictive models to better understand student outcomes. By utilizing algorithms, AI can gain insights into student behavior, helping educators to become more effective in teaching diverse student populations and developing ways to close the gaps that prevent certain students from reaching their full potential. By anticipating individual needs, educators can create curricula that more closely align with a student's interests and areas of need. AI-powered strategies can also help to reduce bias when it comes to grading students and provide more targeted instruction to those students who need help the most.

When it comes to personalized learning, AI-powered strategies can help to facilitate an environment where everyone succeeds. With the right tools, teachers can modify course materials on the fly and tailor instruction for each student's individual learning style. Through AI-powered programs, teachers are able to gain better insight into how each student learns, allowing educators to design a more customized classroom experience. Additionally, AI-powered strategies can help teachers to more effectively respond in real-time to a student's behavior or performance.

Aside from providing a more personalized learning experience, AI-powered strategies for the classroom can also help to reduce student absences, making it easier for a student to make up missed classes or catch up on new material. AI-based programs can automate administrative tasks like attendance-taking, grading, and even assigning homework, freeing up a teacher's time and allowing them to focus on teaching.

AI-powered strategies in the classroom can also create a more entertaining learning experience, as students can interact with animated characters or games in order to better understand course materials. These visual tools not only capture a student's attention, but they allow educators to track their progress and promote deeper engagement. AI can also detect patterns in student interactions, offering tailored feedback that motivates students to stay engaged and perform at their best.

To ensure the success of an AI-powered classroom, educators must first create a culture of learning that supports the use of AI strategies. When students are given the opportunity to participate and collaborate with AI-based activities and strategize their own learning plans, they discover the importance of ownership in their learning experience. This ownership helps to build a stronger sense of self-efficacy and responsibility, fostering a classroom dynamic where everyone learns together and succeeds together.

AI-powered strategies have the potential to transform not only the classroom experience but the outcomes of any student's education. By incorporating AI-powered strategies for the classroom, students gain a more personalized and engaging experience that caters to individual needs and interests. With AI, educators have the tools to create an environment where all students have an equal opportunity to succeed.

Chapter 29: "Harnessing the Power of AI for Personalized Learning in the Classroom"

Harnessing the Power of AI for Personalized Learning in the Classroom is an exciting prospect for educators. Today's classrooms are packed with diverse students with different interests, learning styles, and abilities. Meeting the demands of the 21st Century requires educators to utilize the best available technology to engage each of these unique individuals. Artificial Intelligence (AI) offers the potential to provide personalized learning experiences in the classroom.

AI technology is powered by a combination of data-driven algorithms and machine learning systems. These systems are able to analyze vast amounts of data to generate insights and predictions that allow educators to tailor their instruction to the needs of individual students. AI technology can be used to power personalized learning applications that are customized to each students' unique needs and interests.

Integrating AI in the classroom has the potential to drastically improve the learning experience of each student. Instead of focusing on the teacher as the primary source of knowledge, AI can enable students to learn in ways that are right for them. For example, AI-powered applications can generate dedicated learning paths for each student, providing tailored content and activities. AI tools can also adjust the complexity of the learning material to the level of proficiency of each student, ensuring that each one is challenged but never overwhelmed.

AI-powered applications can also provide personalized feedback to students based on their performance. This feedback can be tailored to the unique requirements and needs of each student. For the educator, this means that instead of spending time providing individual feedback to each student, they can tailor feedback at scale using AI tools. This allows them to focus on providing higher-level guidance for students.

AI-based technologies can be used to track in real-time the progress of each student, allowing educators to quickly identify and intervene with students who are behind on their learning goals. This can dramatically improve the learning outcomes for students by minimizing the learning gaps between them.

The AI-driven classroom also has the potential to open up new possibilities for educators. For example, AI technologies can provide a wealth of data to educators. This data can be used to gain insights into students' learning behavior, interests, and performance. Educators can use this data to improve the efficiency and effectiveness of their instruction, enabling them to provide real time feedback to students and organize large amounts of content.

Harnessing the power of AI for personalized learning in the classroom has the potential to revolutionize the way we teach. This technology can enable educators to provide each student personalized learning paths with relevant content, tailored feedback, and real-time performance tracking. Not only does this create the potential for more effective instruction and increased student engagement, but it can also open up entirely new possibilities for educators.

Chapter 30: "Harnessing AI to Deliver Personalized Learning: Strategies for Success in the Classroom"

There is no doubt that Artificial Intelligence (AI) has the potential to revolutionize the way we teach and learn in classrooms across the world. As AI-powered tools become increasingly available and affordable for teachers, it is important to consider how to make use of AI to deliver personalized learning experiences to our students. Personalized learning refers to a student-centered approach in which instruction is tailored to address an individual's particular learning needs and interests. By harnessing AI, teachers can create more personalized and effective learning experiences that will help students develop the knowledge and skills they will need to succeed in the 21st century.

The first step in harnessing AI for personalized learning is to utilize data collected from student feedback and performance. By collecting data on a student's progress and preferences, AI can be used to create unique learning paths adapted to the individual. AI can also analyze the data to identify any areas where the student may be struggling or gaps in their knowledge. Based on this analysis, AI can suggest targeted materials or activities for the student to help them better understand a given subject. This type of personalized instruction can provide valuable support and guidance for students as they work to develop new skills and knowledge.

Using data to create personalized learning paths, AI can also be used to generate educational resources tailored to an individual's interests and goals. AI-driven personalized recommendations can provide students with tailored materials and activities that are tailored to their individual needs. For example, AI-generated recommendations can identify online courses or books related to a student's interests or recommend a teacher-led project that aligns with their goals. These types of resources can help students find the extra support they need to reach their educational goals.

Another key strategy for creating personalized learning experiences with AI is through educational gamification. AI-powered educational games can be designed to challenge students to solve specific problems or complete specific tasks. By introducing elements of competition and reward, these games provide an engaging and stimulating learning experience. AI-generated rewards and feedback can also help to motivate students and provide positive reinforcement of their progress.

AI can be used to create virtual teaching assistants that can provide additional support and guidance to students during their learning journey. AI-based teaching assistants can offer personalized advice and feedback to help students develop their skills and knowledge. AI-driven tutoring technology can also be used to assess a student's progress and suggest personalized learning activities. By providing personalized guidance and support, AI-driven assistants can help students make significant progress and achieve their academic goals.

Implementing AI for personalized learning is an exciting opportunity that can be used to improve the quality of education for our students. By utilizing the data collected from student feedback and performance, AI-powered personalized recommendations, educational games, and virtual teaching assistants, teachers can create more effective and personalized learning experiences for their students. With the right strategies in place, AI can have a transformational impact on teaching and learning in the classroom.

Don't miss out!

Visit the website below and you can sign up to receive emails whenever Adam Smith publishes a new book. There's no charge and no obligation.

https://books2read.com/r/B-A-OSAW-MAUJC

BOOKS 2 READ

Connecting independent readers to independent writers.

Also by Adam Smith

AI in K-12 Education
Intelligent Machines in the Classroom: Unlocking the Potential of AI in K12 Education
The Future of Learning: Artificial Intelligence in K12 Education
Towards an AI-Infused Revolution in K12 Education
Unleashing AI in the Classroom: Strategies for Implementing Intelligent Technologies in K-12 Education
Unleashing the Potential of Artificial Intelligence in K-12 Education: Reimagining How Learning Happens

Breaking Down Bad Habits
Breaking Down Bad Habits: How to Overcome Self-Defeating Behaviors and Achieve Success

Standalone
Brain Dead: When It Comes To Improving Mental Health, What The Hell Are We Waiting For?
40 Things Intelligent People Do Daily
The Beginner's Guide to Quantum Computing & Mechanics
Open Source AI

Watch for more at https://books2read.com/adamsmith.

About the Author

Adam Smith is a native North Texas Entrepreneur, AI educational expert, and educator who graduated from Embry Riddle University with a Bachelor of Science in Aerospace Studies. In 2007 he co-founded TeacherTube.com, an online education platform community that provides an educationally focused, safe venue for teachers, schools, and home learners. Under his leadership, in September of 2017, a publicly traded company, Salem Media Group, acquired TeacherTube.

After the acquisition, Adam continued his passion for technology and education by helping schools and start-ups to large corporations with digital consulting.

Read more at https://books2read.com/adamsmith.

A. SMITH
MEDIA
Publishing Division | Texas

About the Publisher

A. Smith Media is a fully integrated digital media and distribution company specializing in producing and marketing television, film, home entertainment, music, and interactive games. A. Smith Media has been at the forefront of the commercial growth of Digital Distribution and Internet Video on Demand services through its pioneering efforts in web TV.